Published by EDITO Publishing Agency (Verona Province)
Drawings by Stefania Zanini (Bussolengo, Verona Province)
Photographs by ARC EN CIEL (Verona Province), and DEMETRA Archive

Text adapted from "Cultivating Bonsai" by V. Tridi, Demetra Srl [Limited Liability Company]

Library of Congress Cataloging-in-Publication Data Available

10 9 8 7 6 5 4 3 2

Published by Sterling Publishing Company, Inc.
387 Park Avenue South, New York, N.Y. 10016
First published in Italy
Under the title Coltiviamo i Bonsai
©1998 by Demetra S.r.l.
Via Strà 167, 37030 Colognola ai Colli (VR), Italy
English translation ©2000 by Sterling Publishing
387 Park Avenue South, New York, N.Y. 10016
Distributed in Canada by Sterling Publishing
c/o Canadian Manda Group, One Atlantic Avenue, Suite 105
Toronto, Ontario, Canada M6K 3E7
Distributed in Great Britain and Europe by Cassel PLC
Wellington House, 125 Strand, London WC2R 0BB, England
Distributed in Australia by Capricorn Link (Australia) Pty Ltd.
P.O. BOX 704, Windsor NSW 2756, Australia
Printed in Italy
All rights reserved

Sterling ISBN 0-8069-2879-4

cultivating
bonsai

A special thanks to **TIZIANO ZANINI** of the Bonsai Club in Bussolengo (Verona Province) for kindly making himself available during photo shoots, and for his essential assistance in the revision of the text for this new edition.

A special thanks to Flover garden center
(Bussolengo, Verona Province)
for their enthusiasm and assistance
in the production of images.

Via Pastrengo, 16
Bussolengo (Verona Province)
Tel: (045) 675-9511
Fax: (045) 670-1782

TABLE OF CONTENTS

AN ANCIENT ART

The term "bonsai" is not merely a term for a small tree grown in a small pot, but also an art and style of life that developed in China many centuries ago. Chinese bonsai masters made a distinction between *pun-sai* and *pun-ching*. The first term is repeated in the sound and content of the later Japanese term *bonsai* (from *bon*, "tray, container" and *sai*, "to cultivate"). On the other hand, *pun-ching* was used to mean a tree planted in a container and surrounded by a landscape.

In any event, prior to becoming a merely aesthetic expression, bonsai was conceived as the desire to achieve harmony between the sky and earth, between man and nature – a profound spiritual force capable of expressing moods ranging from intimate to sublime

in a perfect act. The decision made by Ton Guen-Ming, a famous poet and officer of the Chinese army, should be seen in this aura of mysticism: after abandoning state matters, he decided to lead a pleasant life cultivating chrysanthemums in pots. This probably may have been the first step towards cultivating not only flowers but also trees in small containers.

Around the year one thousand, the *pun-sai* earned their place in literary descriptions, and this art, which was initially the prerogative of nobility, became a privilege of all Chinese social classes starting in the second half of the 17th century.

In Japan, bonsai made their appearance as a gift that Chinese noblemen gave to Japanese ambassadors, and then they spread further as a result of the work of merchants. In Japan, bonsai at first became an art for aristocrats cultivated with the same degree of spiritual intensity as the Chinese masters. Then in the second half of the 19th century it was "opened up" to the public.

In 1878, thanks to a Japanese exhibitor that participated in the World's Fair in Paris, bonsai also spread to Europe.

Whether in the form of a single tree or a grove of trees, bonsai should conjure up an image of trees in their natural environment in the minds of those who look at them. The ultimate goal of this art is to witness the slow changes of nature by suggesting a feeling of inner peace, calm and simplicity.

FIRST CONTACT WITH BONSAI

The first step to be taken is to decide which plant to acquire. For the novice, it is never easy to decide which plant will be most suitable for bonsai. Frequently he will be attracted by a specimen that is full of leaves or has heavy flowering, but he will fail to note that the bonsai, in the first case, would be deprived of a conical shape, and in the second case, would have few branches.

Anyone desiring to raise bonsai must, first and foremost, learn to look at a potential specimen from the standpoint of harmony avoiding anything that could otherwise be a source of enormous, but short-lived, satisfaction.

Specimens for sale come in various sizes. To be specific, they can be divided into five groups based on height (varying from a minimum of 7 cm to a maximum of just over 120 cm):

▶ **Miniature bonsai**, the smallest in size reaching a maximum size of 15 cm;

▶ **Small bonsai**, less than 22 cm in height, and the most commonly available for sale;

▶ **Small-medium bonsai**, with a height between 20 and 40 cm;

▶ **Medium bonsai**, consisting of specimens with a height of between 40 and 90 cm, and representing the most common bonsai in collections;

▶ **Large bonsai** reaching (and at times exceeding) a height of 120 cm.

The height of a bonsai should be calculated by measuring from the top of the plant to the rim of its container, whatever the form of the container and style of the tree.

The term "bonsai" is reserved only for specimens raised that truly convey the impression of a real miniature tree to the observer. Until this is achieved, the end result will merely be a small plant with good features that must still be trained and cared for to achieve the desired goal.

BONSAI STYLES

Through its various forms, the art of bonsai attempts to imitate what can be seen in nature. Just as nature varies and changes plants by presenting them in forms, groups and multiple adaptations, bonsai can be expressed in different styles and interpretations. Leaving aside the concept that no two bonsai are exactly alike, we will attempt to classify the main styles of this art in general terms.

INDIVIDUAL BONSAI

In this paragraph, we cover the main forms that an individual plant can assume, and we provide the corresponding Japanese term for each.

MOYOGI
OR INFORMAL UPRIGHT STYLE

This style, more than any others, generally approximates the natural adaptation of plants, and thus, it is the easiest to execute.

The vertical line of the trunk is straight but with a winding appearance that makes the form appear more natural. The tree, moreover, is in perfect balance with the top, which is in line with the base of the trunk.

Branches are distributed in an alternating and relaxed manner. The leading branch is always the largest, while others get smaller going up towards the top of the plant.

To fully enjoy flowering, it is often necessary to let the bonsai go "outside its form." Later, maintenance pruning will be used after flowering has ended.

For the formation of this style, we will initially avoid pruning excessively so the plant will not become too weak, and we will only eliminate the larger branches towards the top of the trunk.

The species most suitable for the moyogi style are oaks, maples and beeches.

Although it is the most common of bonsai styles, the formal upright style (below) can be pleasantly personalized to suit your imagination.

In the informal upright style (at left) the trunk dominates over the other parts of the plant.

CHOKKAN
OR FORMAL UPRIGHT STYLE

This style is distinguished by a single trunk that tapers gradually towards the top. The largest branches spread out in a regular pattern from the base in a symmetrical and balanced manner. Thick superficial roots are arranged in a circular pattern, and the entire plant consists of a well-proportioned conical shape.

Starting at the base of the trunk, the exact sequence of branches requires the largest branch to be positioned to the right or left of the observer, the second branch just above the first on the opposite side, the third branch just above the second on the opposite side, and so on, continually getting smaller until an ideal conical shape is formed.

As in the case of *moyogi*, branches must develop parallel to the ground, and to achieve this, you will need to use wire binding. Obviously pruning will be used to eliminate branches that are not growing in harmony with the shape. This is to be done with pruning shears with curved blades that will cut the branch creating a concave area at the point of insertion with the trunk allowing the bark to grow and cover the wound.

> *The species most suitable for the* chokkan *style are conifers.*

SHAKAN
OR SLANT STYLE

The trunk of the plant is slanted at various angles to the ground. This style is not arranged in a continuous pattern due to its divided form from which branches grow that are more or less vigorous and dense.

This style is similar to *fukinagashi* (and is often confused with it), but differs from it in the form of branches that grow in all directions. Roots are large and visible on

In the slant style, the base of the trunk and the trunk itself must give an impression of power in opposition to the slant of the foliage.

In the semi-cascade style, the tree seems to fight with all its strength against the powers of nature that attempt to bend and destroy it.

the surface of the soil and positioned in the direction of the plant's slant. The lower treetop never goes beyond the base of the pot.

KENGAI
OR FULL CASCADE STYLE

This style is an artistic imitation of the appearance of trees growing under special environmental conditions such as steep precipices blown by the wind. The main feature of this style is the arched trunk bent over itself and leaving the container to form a cascade of growth. The branches are positioned in alternating fashion in such a way that the base branch is directed towards the center of the container to counterbalance the scenic impact of the other branches that cascade below.

For this style very deep and tall containers are used that are usually placed on a stool or high, narrow table to accentuate the scenic impact of the trunk's flow and to facilitate pruning.

The *kengai* style comes in many varieties such as the typical "weeping branch waterfall."

Nothing in nature – snow, rocks, landslides – can stop a tree's will to live. Thus, in the kengai style, a tree adapts to the ruggedness of the precipice on which it is located.

Zelkova nire
in semi-cascade style:
It will take a few years for the
overhanging effect to become more
evident and to fall correctly as a
result of regular pruning procedures.

**The placement of this
specimen in the pot**
is excellent. The difference between
it and the cascade style illustrated
below is evident.

The trees best suited for the kengai *style
are conifers, azaleas,* Cotoneaster,
hawthorns and quinces.

Han-Kengai
OR SEMI-CASCADE STYLE

This style is very similar to the previous style (from which it takes part of its name), but differs from it in that its trunk, which falls outside the container, stops its fall just below the rim of the pot, curves gently downward and then rises almost immediately.

The trees best suited for the han-kengai *style are the same ones listed for the* kengai *style.*

THE GROWTH
OF A PLANT

The development of a tree depends on two factors: the elongation and increase in diameter of its various parts. Elongation can only occur for a limited period, i.e., while the parts are still shoots. In fact, as soon as the lignification process starts, the part (whether the trunk or branches) immediately stops developing.

On the other hand, the diameter of the trunk and branches continues to grow for the entire life of the plant (although at different rates). Thus, at the time the structure of a specimen is determined, it is necessary to bear in mind that it will remain the same for the entire life of the tree. Only the proportions of the parts can change as the plant gradually grows.

GROUP BONSAI

This second group includes bonsai styles that are formed from several trunks originating from the same root, and styles planted in groups. Before reviewing the various styles, we should recall that the Japanese have little fondness for symmetry. Accordingly, anyone desiring to strictly adhere to the principles of

cultivating bonsai must avoid making groups consisting of even numbers (with the exception of the number two).

SOKAN, OR TWIN TRUNK STYLE

The *sokan* style is the most elementary form in this second group of bonsai styles. It consists of the development of two trunks of differing diameters (the thicker trunk is called the "father," and the slimmer trunk, the "son") from the same root.

Frequently a second tree will grow at the base of another tree and will be a little smaller, but in harmony with the main specimen. This is the case with bonsai trained in the twin trunk style.

To achieve the right aesthetic effect, the point separating the trunks must be as low as possible, thereby creating the effect of two completely independent trees growing close together just by chance.

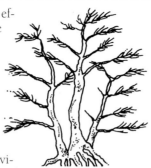

SANKAN OR MULTIPLE TRUNK STYLE

This is a variation of the previous style. It differs from the *sokan* style in that three trunks come from the same root instead of two.

To stand out aesthetically, these trees must also be of different sizes: the more developed is called the "father," the smallest, "the son," and the medium-size tree is called the "mother."

KABUDACHI OR CLUMP STYLE

This is another variation of the *sokan* style. Using root shoots that branch off from the same root, an unspecific number of trunks can be grown.

In the multiple trunk style, the effect is duplicated of several specimens growing from the same stump (for example, see the photograph of the pine on page 13).

The raft style produces a definite impact by simulating a tree knocked down by the force of the wind or by the weight of snow, and from the trunk of which new specimens grow.

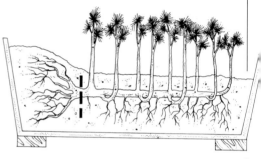

IKADA OR RAFT STYLE

This is one of the most appealing group bonsai styles in the form of a trunk fallen on its side that has given life to new vegetation.

To execute this style correctly, a seedling must be chosen that has dense branches on one side, and little branching on the other. Once weak branches have been removed and the others positioned in the right direction, place the trunk horizontally in a long tray that can accommodate it fully including the root structure. Once the trunk is covered with soil, the branches will stick up vertically giving the impression of a minor plant tragedy with a strong romantic flavor: A tree has broken up on the ground, and once in contact with the ground, it rooted, and its branches became several trunks that continued to thrive. Remember to

In the clump style, the number of trunks must always be greater than three, and always an odd number.

check root formation every six months by removing a bit of soil around the trunk. Once this has occurred and a strong and dense root structure has formed, the former roots can be removed carefully. If, over time, the old trunk has a tendency to rise up from the ground, secure it with a U-shaped section of wire.

Little stones, rocks, grass and musk contribute to the realism of the group planting style.

YOSE-UE
OR GROUP PLANTING STYLE

In the *yose-ue* style, trees of different ages and heights are planted together to suggest the image of a forest or woods. In this case, the number of specimens must also be odd, but what is more important is their position in the tray: In fact, in the space of a few square centimeters, a bonsai enthusiast will try to reproduce a scene, from nature.

To be successful in this minor miracle, perspective, foreshortening and the use of plants of different sizes must be used.

NETSURANARI
OR RAFT FROM SINUOUS ROOT STYLE

This is a variation of the *ikada* style. In this case thick trunks are conceived from a single trunk and root laid out in a crooked pattern on the soil to increase the scenic impact.

To achieve this style, we will follow the same procedure for the normal raft style, with the sole embellishment of selecting a specimen with a sinuous trunk.

The profound effect of working with bonsai comes from the work one does with the winding style of the trunk.

The trees best suited for the yose-ue style are bamboo, Zelkova, cypresses, spruce firs, pines...

15

BONSAI STYLES FOR GROUPS

► When positioning plants in the container, always keep in mind the vantage point from which the arrangement will be appreciated to avoid the mistake of hiding one tree behind another.

► Before position the trees in a pot, make a sketch to determine the position of each tree with precision.

► Place larger trees in front, medium-size trees in the next level, and small trees in the back. This foreshortening will make it possible to give a perspective depth to the bonsai arrangement.

► Remember that when assembling a bonsai in the group planting style, the position of empty space is as important as that of the trees themselves.

► Use pots of different shapes provided they are low and elongated.

► When planting, it is necessary to place a piece of fine wire mesh (over the drain hole) on the bottom of the pot. Then, a thin layer of gravel must be spread to facilitate water drainage, and on top of this, an equally thin layer of special bonsai soil must be spread.

► After positioning the trees according to the sketch, fill the empty spaces between trees with additional bonsai soil taking care to press it down firmly, especially around the edges.

► If you wish, you can now cover the soil with moss which, in addition to conserving moisture, also serves as an embellishment.

► Once planting is completed, water the plants lightly and carefully, and then place the container in a shady spot protected from the wind.

► Wait a full month to gradually get the bonsai used to direct sunlight. However, wait a few more weeks before spreading a small amount of fertilizer.

A bonsai grove represents a major achievement for bonsai enthusiasts. This is because a single container contains the skilled execution of many concepts and immeasurable ingenuity. In addition, in all likelihood the first bonsai were like the ones illustrated here: miniature bamboo groves living in harmony.

Old specimen of Ficus panda raised in the multiple trunk style from a single stump. Pruning is required to show off its structure.

BONSAI STYLES FOR GROUPS AND INDIVIDUAL TREES

This third group looks at styles that are suited are to single bonsai as opposed to group compositions. Let's look at the main shapes.

BUNJING OR LITERATI STYLE

The name of this style probably comes from the fact that bonsai formed in this style are very similar to the trees depicted in ancient Chinese paintings.

In bonsai of the literary (or literati) style, the trunk grows upright or at a slight incline, with no branches except at the top where a few well-formed branches make

In the literati style, the foliage is reduced to the bare minimum. Thus, only the vegetation that is absolutely necessary to prevent the plant from dying is maintained.

up the foliage. The size of the plant is disproportionate to the size of the pot. The latter is usually small and can barely hold the root structure.

HOKIDACHI
OR UPSIDE-DOWN BROOM[1] STYLE

In this style, which favors the growth of lateral shoots, branches are trained into a shape similar to an upside-down broom. In addition to being sturdy, the root structure must be distributed in a harmonious pattern at the base of the trunk. There is one variation of the *hokidachi* style that requires the gradual removal of branches from an area a little more than half-way up the trunk to the top. The specimens that adapt best to this style are those originating from cuttings or layering. In fact, it is difficult to find young specimens in nature with suitable characteristics.

Olea europea [Olive] trained in the upside-down broom style. This specimen has a trunk with a good cone shape.

> The species that are most suited to the hokidachi *style are the elm, oak, birch and Zelkova. For the latter, however, it will be necessary to apply wire to orient branches in the desired direction.*

FUKINAGASHI
OR WINDSWEPT STYLE

This is undoubtedly one of the most sensational bonsai styles due to the realism of the forms representing it. As in the case of the *shakan* style, the trunk has a pronounced slant, but in contrast to

In the upside-down broom style, foliage is trained to form a "capillary" branch network that is particularly apparent during the winter, and serves as a reminder of the species commonly found in our rural areas.

Garden centers are frequently the first point of contact with the bonsai world: these places make it possible to admire various specimens, resolve any initial doubts and satisfy our curiosity..

that style, branches point in a single direction and are all inserted on the slanted side of the trunk. This accentuates the notion of a tree shaped by gusts of wind that beat against the cliff tops.

To achieve this style, you must remove all branches growing "against the wind," while those in the correct position must cover most of the trunk and develop in such a way to give the structure a realistic quality. The roots, as in the case of the majority of other styles, must appear to be well developed to convey the idea of the resistance that the plant musters against the forces of nature.

The trees best suited for the fukinagashi *style are those that grow tall such as pines, yews and junipers...*

In the fukinagashi *style the plant's foliage appears to be shaped by the force of the wind.*

The clinging-to-rock style is definitely one of the most enchanting bonsai styles.

ISHITSUKI OR CLINGING TO ROCK STYLE

A tree growing on a rock is an evocative image that could not escape the world of bonsai. There are various ways of managing the rock-bonsai relationship, but all are based on two fundamental methods.

The first of these sets the tree as the dominant element on the scene. The tree clutches the rocky fragment with its roots as if to crush it. The second method completely reverses the relationship. Now the rock is in the prominent position, barely able to accommodate the tiny trees growing here and there on its surface. From a technical standpoint, it is important to note that in the first case the roots, properly positioned in a circular pattern, descend along the rock until dropping to the container. In the second situation, the rock is much larger and the roots are required to grow in small cavities in which soil is placed.

There are other variations of these two models. For example, certain roots may take part of their nutrients from the soil in the container, and part from the cavities in the rocks. Still other bonsai are positioned at the base of rock fragments. Your taste will dictate which position is best suited for the plants you have. Here, then, are the methods for the proper execution of the *ishitsuki* style on a rock and the same style in a rock corresponding to the two styles we just defined.

ISHITSUKI ON A ROCK

Follow these directions if you want a bonsai with uncovered roots, or a tree whose long roots dominate the rock and drop down to the soil in the pot.

▶ First, select a suitable specimen at a nursery, or gather one yourself.

▶ After removing the soil around the roots with a stick, carefully position the plant on the rock that will accommodate the plant, and distribute the root structure in a tasteful and harmonious manner. Remove any roots that are too big, too small, or out of place.

▶ Drop root tips down to the soil and cover the roots on the rock with a thin layer of protective soil half of which is clay, and the other half is peat. This layer will serve to feed and protect the plant during the first phase of the plant's adaptation.

TIPS FOR CLINGING TO ROCK STYLE

In this style it is necessary to achieve close harmony between two very different but complementary materials (the rock and the plant). These two elements must always be of different sizes so that one of them may dominate the other. It is possible to find ketosushi for sale, which is a highly malleable Japanese soil. Once it sticks to the rock, it will not come off, even during watering.

▶ To repeat, once the roots have been arranged according to your taste, they may be secured to the rock in various ways. You can affix the roots by binding them with raffia fiber or tape, or with thin metal wire that you can anchor to the cavities of the rock with small pieces of lead that can be wedged in place using a hammer and chisel.

If need be, you can also drill holes in the rock and thread wire through the holes. However, this is a rather laborious process and should be used only if absolutely necessary.

▶ After removing excess anchoring wire, place a layer of peat and clay on the roots, approximately 1-centimeter-thick, and

When preparing the clinging-to-rock style bonsai, after anchoring the plant (see the sequence shown in the drawings), it is very important to cover the root structure with soil, and try to insert as much material as possible in the various cracks of the base used.

▶ Once this procedure has been completed, the plant will be very weak and will need attention, partially due to the small amount of soil in which it is forced to live. This will require constant watering in small amounts as soon as the top layer of soil looks dry. The muslin and bog moss can be removed in 5-6 months once the bonsai has formed a sufficient root structure in the tray.

cover with bog moss that should be affixed with strips of muslin.

▶ Finally, arrange the clinging-to-rock style bonsai in an appropriate container taking care to completely cover root tips that will provide nourishment for the plant in the future.

ISHITSUKI IN A ROCK

The following method should be used for clinging-to-rock style bonsai whose roots cling to the natural or artificial cavities of the rock.

8 RULES
FOR CLINGING-TO-ROCK STYLE BONSAI

▶ A basic rule for achieving a pleasing aesthetic result from a clinging-to-rock style bonsai is to never use trees and rocks that are the same size.

▶ For your first experience, use trees that have already been trained. If the tree is to have the dominant role, obtain specimens with an excellent root structure.

▶ You should still make several sketches in advance of the project you wish to carry out.

▶ For the rock base, look for rocks with heightened coloring and evocative shapes, and avoid gray and uniform rocks.

▶ If a rock has pleasing features but no places for anchoring, this can be remedied with a little chisel work.

▶ To prepare the front of the rock, always select the best perspective. In this regard, remember that bonsai can be used to represent various locations: a mountain, a jagged coastline, an island, an enormous fragment of fallen rock, or merely small rocks on top of which your tree decided to grow.

▶ When choosing the type of plant to use, keep in mind that conifers should usually be positioned in high places.

▶ The most appropriate pots for clinging-to-rock style bonsai are shallow and oval. They should not be showy, or the arrangement will not be prominent. The color of the pot should also follow this rule. Accordingly, neutral tones are the best. Based on what you are trying to depict, the flat space from which the rock "rises" in the pot may be covered with sand or even water if the intent is to depict a beach or the sea.

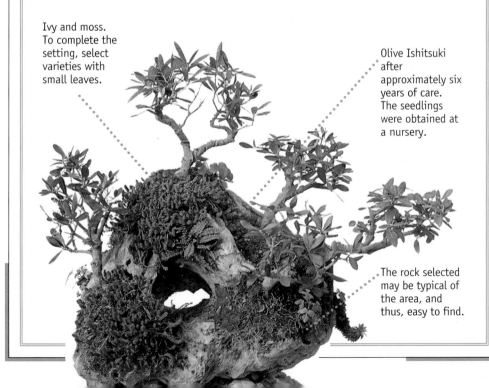

Ivy and moss. To complete the setting, select varieties with small leaves.

Olive Ishitsuki after approximately six years of care. The seedlings were obtained at a nursery.

The rock selected may be typical of the area, and thus, easy to find.

HOW TO DEVELOP A GOOD ROOT STRUCTURE

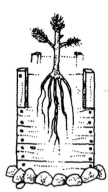

We have already explained that a bonsai in the clinging-to-rock style requires a perfect and well-developed root structure that will be positioned harmoniously to cover the surface of the rock, and will descend to absorb nutrients from the soil.

The plant to be trained for this style may be found in nature, at a nursery, or created artificially. If necessary, to obtain a plant with long and well-developed roots, it is sufficient to grow the future ishitsuki in a very deep plastic pot filled with a mix of peat and sand. Starting at the top, every 3-4 months remove a (4-5 cm) portion of the upper edge of the pot, gradually exposing the root structure. This will cause the root structure to develop quickly and deeply to replace roots exposed by removing the covering layer.

By continuing to regularly remove the upper part of the pot, after 12-18 months you will have a plant with a long, well-developed root structure, and with the arrival of spring, you can use it to create a bonsai in the clinging-to-rock style.

In addition to the ishitsuki style, the development of a long root structure can also be used for the creation of a pleasing bonsai with above-ground roots.

▶ After identifying the depressions that are best suited for positioning your bonsai, clean them, and if necessary, enlarge them with a drill or chisel.

▶ With regard to anchoring, following the same procedure for bonsai with exposed roots: Affix supporting wires with small pieces of hammered lead or use the technique of threading wire through small holes made with appropriate drills. At the end of the procedure, moisten the cavities with water.

▶ Using a small stick, remove the soil from the plant's roots and position it in the prepared rock cavity in which you have spread a layer of soil. Using a mix of peat and soil, cover the root structure of the bonsai.

▶ Using extreme care, anchor the plant with copper or aluminum wire, and place the bonsai in a suitable container, keeping it out of the wind and in dim light.

▶ In this case the *ishitsuki* will also require tremendous patience, and once again, the greatest problem will be the need to keep it constantly moist. When watering, make sure to distribute water only around the root structure.

▶ After a couple of months, you may give the plant its first portion of organic fertilizer in liquid form using extremely small amounts.

▶ In contrast to the previous type of bonsai, this type should not be transplanted, and roots should not be trimmed.

Obvious defect in the twisting of the branch resulting from leaving the binding wire on for too long.

Ishitsuki on rock in the form of a Japanese maple. Excellent overall effect.

With the passage of time and the care of the bonsai enthusiast, the rock and plant have become an integral unit.

MINIATURE LANDSCAPES

The depiction of a scene from nature, or a miniature landscape, is called *saikei* in Japanese.

In this type of bonsai, we not only find groups of trees, trees planted on rocks and depictions of wooded islands, but also all the styles covered on previous pages are used and combined based on refined arrangement techniques that are used to form a landscape that appears to have come from a fourteenth century Chinese painting. The materials used to decorate these delicate scenes include trees of various types, forms and ages; rocks; soils; and sometimes, even small houses and statues of animals and men.

Naturally, all these elements must be positioned in the arrangement in a harmonious or contrasting manner depending on the type of landscape desired (pastoral, wild, seascape, etc.), and this is where the art of the bonsai enthusiast becomes apparent. It is not based as much on the quantity of articles included in the arrangement, as it is on the pathos aroused by each of these in relation to the others. Thus, rather than attempt to find the perfect rock or tree, the main goal will be to achieve an overall effect. The topsoil will play an essential role: It will be used to create artificial elevations that give energy to the scene and hide any imperfections of the arrangement.

When the trees used in the *saikei* start growing and disturb the balance of the landscape, they must be identified and replaced with other specimens. Among other things, this too is a particularly interesting aspect. *Saikei* are landscapes that are never static and are constantly changing with the addition and removal of items. Very shallow containers in neutral colors must be chosen: In fact, containers serve only as supports, and must be as inconspicuous as possible.

With regard to placement, follow a basic layout by first positioning the rocks, and then the trees (which are fastened to the bottom of the container or placed on the rocks like *ishitsuki*).

The overall effect will be completed with nutrient-rich soil, dirt or sand to balance the basic elements of the landscape. As in the case of all bonsai, *saikei* should also be kept out of the wind and watered periodically.

A fisherman, a pagoda and two people sitting: These are some of the elements that can transform your bonsai into a slice of everyday life.

What could be better than sipping tea in the shade of a false cypress tree as a "fortune teller" passes by, and an oriental bonsai gardener works on a plant?

MINIATURE BONSAI

This definition is used for tiny trees of an exceptionally small size, usually measuring less than 15 cm in height. You can obtain seedlings in the spring in the woods. Once you have identified a specimen (a seedling no taller than 5 cm), remove it from the ground without damaging the root structure, which must be wrapped in a damp cloth so it will not dry out.

The soil base that nourishes a miniature bonsai must be refined in structure and kept moist constantly. For this reason, it is necessary to water often, with more frequent watering in the summer. Plants must be fertilized once weekly, but given the small size of the containers, it may be appropriate to apply fertilizer using a syringe through the drainage hole.

Since seedlings are extremely small in size, it will be difficult to regulate their development using ordinary wire binding. Thus, it is better to rely primarily on pruning. In the beginning, prune 1-2 buds from the small plants, and repeat the procedure as often as necessary. Then let a few branches grow while still maintaining the shape desired, removing any unnecessary branches with your fingers.

Since the growth area is limited, miniature bonsai need to be repotted more than normal bonsai. At the time of each repotting procedure, remove one third of the length of the root structure, and for varieties that have heavy foliage, remove approximately one half of all leaves. Once the transplant is complete, take care to protect the bonsai from the sun, and keep it in a shady protected area for about ten days.

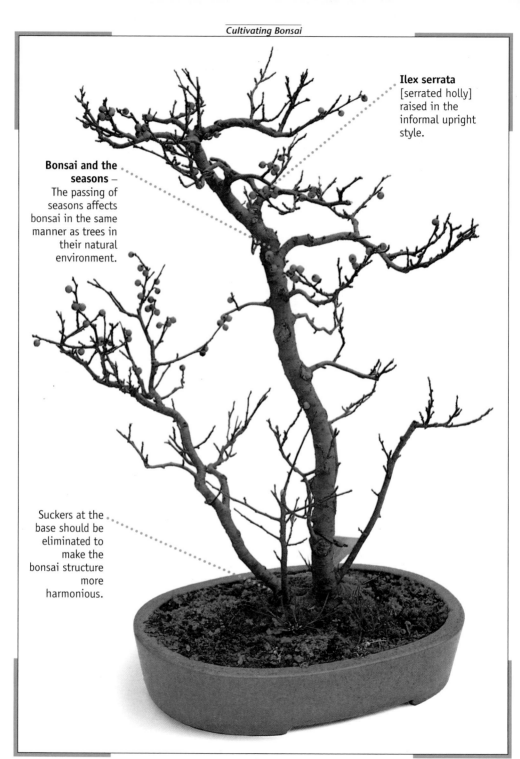

Ilex serrata [serrated holly] raised in the informal upright style.

Bonsai and the seasons – The passing of seasons affects bonsai in the same manner as trees in their natural environment.

Suckers at the base should be eliminated to make the bonsai structure more harmonious.

CREATING A BONSAI

After reviewing the various styles and types of bonsai, we will now look at how to obtain a seedling to be used for our purposes. In the following pages, we review the various methods for reproducing plants.

However, it should be noted that it is also possible to obtain a plant by making a selection from the specimens available at a **nursery** and then shaping it according to our wishes. This alternative seems to be the most suited for someone who is just getting started, since there are healthy, vigorous plants to use for initial attempts. Look closely at the plants available and don't hurry. Also, focus on specimens that most resemble the style you want to achieve. The decision to obtain a bonsai that is already formed (see box below) also seems to be an appropriate choice to meet the needs of the novice. It's up to you.

BONSAI GROWN FROM SEEDS

Reproducing bonsai from seeds is undoubtedly the most natural and complete method for obtaining a plant suitable for bonsai. The time needed to grow a sufficiently developed specimen will be compensated by the

---

BONSAI THAT ARE ALREADY FORMED

The easiest way to obtain bonsai plants is to buy them from a specialized garden center. In this case there is no great personal satisfaction, but time and risks are all but eliminated. When making a purchase, choose trustworthy retailers, and always check the health of the specimens personally. Plants should have roots that spread out and a thick base. The trunk should have a conical form, and bark should be visible. Branches should start about one-third of the way up the plant, and should be larger at the base than the top.

Make this decision responsibly. A bonsai needs constant care, and it is useless to buy one if you don't think you will have the time and attention to devote to it. This would quickly result in its death. On the other hand, if your decision is weighed carefully, we advise you to obtain at least two specimens, perhaps a conifer and a broadleaf. This will allow you to raise two species at the same time with differing needs which will broaden your experience in this field. A further important recommendation: if you do not have a great deal of gardening experience, select varieties that are typical to the area where you live.

Gardens centers with bonsai departments frequently have ties to amateur associations in the area. These are an excellent point of reference for advice, courses, etc.

It is quite easy to find bonsai material without great expense.
It is enough to visit a well supplied nursery and select healthy, well formed plants.

TIPS FOR PLANTING SEEDS

Although this technique requires time and patience, it will be highly satisfying to see your bonsai take shape and grow year after year. During this procedure, seeds must be distributed uniformly over the entire surface of the soil.

Thus, before beginning, calculate the number of seeds to use (based on container size) and the spacing between seeds.

pleasure of cultivating a plant that you have given life to.

▶ You can obtain seeds by gathering them in the wild (but you will have to know how to recognize seeds), or buying them from retailers of your choice. Spring is the best season for planting seeds.

It is important to remember that each type of seed has special needs. In particular, fresh seeds (those just taken from fruit) should immediately be placed in a propagator. Other seeds, however, should be cooled for a period of about 1 month in moist sand or in the refrigerator. Once they have started to germinate, they are ready to be placed in the propagator.

▶ Once you have obtained seeds, prepare the seedbed or propagator. This should be a small disinfected and clean container

The drawing above shows the sequence of training a plant obtained from a seed in the moyogi *style. (At right is an old specimen of* Zelkova nire).

that will be filled with a soil base for germination made up of a mix of soil, sand and peat.

▶ Spread seeds at the correct depth: 2-3 cm for larger seeds, 0.5-1 cm for smaller seeds. As a general rule, bear in mind that the layer used to cover the seeds must be at least equal to the diameter of the seed.

▶ Once seeds have been planted, even out the surface of the propagator using a small rake, and water using a mister of a watering can with an aerator so that the seeds will not be dislodged.

▶ It is a common practice to cover the propagator with a plate of glass or trans-parent plastic to protect the seeds from insects, birds and mice. This protection also takes advantage of the greenhouse effect by keeping the soil warm and maintaining a certain level of humidity.

TRANSPLANTING

The propagator, in which you planted several more seeds than the plants you will need (the ratio is about 1:100), should be placed in a draft free area. As soon as the plants start to germinate, remove the protective plate of glass or plastic, and when the second pair of leaves has sprouted, it will be time to transplant them in a shallow container filled with fine soil.

It takes at least a couple of years for plants to have sufficient development to endure the first bonsai treatment.

BONSAI FROM CUTTINGS

Cuttings, which are used to reproduce a plant from one of its parts (stems, leaves or roots), make it possible to obtain plants similar to the original plant in much less time than it takes to produce a plant from a seed. Below we provide tips for preparing the main types of cuttings.

STEM CUTTINGS

Stem cuttings can be broken down into sprout cuttings, semi-woody cuttings and woody cuttings depending on the consistency of wood.

▶ **Sprout cuttings** use the spring growth of deciduous species such as magnolias, maples, etc.

Small branch cuttings should be gathered between June and July and must be between 7 and 12 cm long. Cuttings should always be removed with their leaves, and their rooting takes place in a very moist environment. Once the small branch has been cut off, all lower leaves should be eliminated, and the tips of higher leaves should be removed to minimize water loss from transpiration. The cuttings, which should be gathered in the early morning, must be kept moist in wet paper or bog

TIPS FOR SHOOT CUTTINGS

For this procedure to be successful, cuttings must be planted immediately after they are removed. To prevent drying, spray them with water at room temperature several times a day.

TIPS FOR SEMI-WOODY CUTTINGS

Try to select a small branch that already has a good basic structure so that as new branches grow, it will be easy to produce a little bonsai.

moss. Before planting, the base should be spread with a solution of hormone rooting powder.

After being prepared as described, the shoots should be planted in a sufficient amount of soil base to cover one third of their length. They should be bent slightly and separated somewhat from one another. The cutting bed, which is where the cuttings will take root and become independent plants, must be placed in an area with a constant temperature (about 18° C), and its soil must be made up of an even mix of inert sand, peat and a certain amount of perlite and bentonite.

▶ **Semi-woody** cuttings should be collected between July and September at the time when shoots turn to wood. These will take longer to root than shoot cuttings.

Remove cuttings approximately 15 cm long from the original plant and eliminate shoots and base leaves halfway up the stem. Then insert one half of the length of

TIPS FOR LEAF CUTTINGS

From the tree's foliage, it is important to select a branch tip that is particularly healthy. This is the only way to assure good root formation.

each cutting in the cutting bed soil, protect them from direct sunlight and water periodically.

▶ Finally, **woody cuttings** should be prepared in the late fall or in the winter when shoots have completely turned to wood (the best sprouts for this purpose are those that are not very vigorous[2] with long distances between leaf nodes and average strength). The length of cuttings will vary between 10 and 25 cm depending on the species.

Trim cuttings into uniform lengths, tie them in bunches with iron wire, and keep them in a cool and moist environment until spring. When planting in the cutting bed, the bunches must be undone, and the individual cuttings must be planted precisely.

LEAF CUTTINGS

This type of cutting is performed by removing a piece of stem with a leaf from the original plant. This will be inserted in properly prepared soil that is quite similar to that described for stem cuttings, with only the leaf protruding above the soil. If watered regularly and protected from direct sunlight, the stem will develop roots and foliage.

ROOT CUTTINGS

This type of reproduction is very simple to do, and works well with trees that naturally reproduce by sending out suckers. The latter are shoots growing on roots that develop externally and form new individual plants. In the winter, collect the roots of the species that you wish to reproduce, and then cut them in 7-8 cm sections. Tie them in bunches and place them in boxes with moist sand at 36-40° Farhenheit until spring. At the proper moment, the cuttings must be transplanted vertically in a suitable location, making sure that the top is positioned even with the surface of the soil.

How to properly remove root cuttings (sections 1 and 2).

BONSAI FROM LAYERING

Layering is a technique that makes it possible to rapidly obtain well-formed specimens that will become future bonsai. This is done by placing a branch from the plant that is to be reproduced in soil or peat in an appropriate container.
To facilitate the sprouting of roots, it is necessary to make an incision or cut in the portion of the branch where it is desired to sprout roots.
The proper time to perform layering is in the spring.
Once a plant has been selected that meets our requirements, a ring of bark is cut on

LAYERING TIPS

Reproducing plants using layering makes it possible to obtain good specimens in relatively short periods (6 – 30 weeks), with the exception of the pine that takes two years. It is important for the portion to be layered to have a good structure since it alone will make up the little bonsai.

35

At right, Before closing the plastic bag covering the layered area, make sure that the bog moss inside the bag is fully moistened. It must be kept moist until rooting has occurred, and especially during summer months.

the selected branch, and is kept open to prevent scarring.

Once the cut has been treated with hormone rooting powder, wrap a polyethylene bag around the incision containing bog moss that must be kept moist.

Now the only thing left to do is to check to make sure the procedure was successful. If after a few weeks the branch has dried out, the procedure has failed. If, however, the branch is sprouting roots in the area of the ring of bark removed, the layering was a success. Wait for the root structure to be well established before cutting the branch just below the roots.

You now have a new plant that is identical to the original plant. Once it is removed from the bog moss, you can move it to a place that is protected from the wind and sun.

After some time, you may plant it permanently, and it will be ready for your care.

Close up of the root structure of a layered plant.
The roots exhibit good capillary development.

BONSAI
FROM GRAFTING

At times grafting techniques may also be useful for bonsai. This practice consists of inserting the part of the plant from which

The foliage on this Chinese elm, which was grafted three years ago, has finally formed and will only need maintenance pruning.

GRAFTING TIPS

If you have a specimen with a good trunk, and you want to raise a bonsai in the upside-down broom style, grafting can be used in addition to pruning to contribute to the formation of foliage. The branches to be grafted must be proportionate to the type of foliage desired. Approximately ten branches removed from a similar species during pruning were grafted to the Chinese elm pictured on this page.

it is desired to obtain foliage (called the graft, scion or *gentile*[3]) on another plant (called the host, *selvatico*[4] or specimen plant) that provides the root structure. A specimen will result with characteristics of both species used. For example, if a variety of apple tree has a strong root structure with low demands, and another variety of apple tree has excellent fruit bearing qualities, grafting them will result in a plant with strong roots and abundant fruit. This may be an overly simplistic example, but it gives a good idea of the grafting concept.

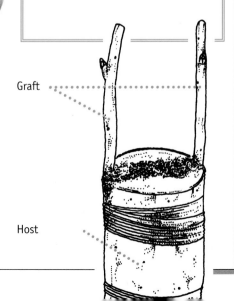

Graft

Host

Returning to bonsai, we can use the grafting technique for our purposes by adapting plants to specific situations.

Usually grafting is done in the spring, when growth reappears on plants, and may be carried out in different ways. There are several common factors, however, that contribute to the success of this technique.

▶ **Similarity of graft and specimen plant:** The two parts that will give life to the new plant must have similar characteristics. You cannot graft an apple tree to a peach tree, but it would be possible to graft a peach tree to an apricot tree since they both belong to the same family.

▶ **Proper positioning of the growing tissue:** The part of the trunk immediately under the bark, which has a vital function in the tree's life, must be positioned properly since sap vessels run through this area. If we graft two parts of different plants, they must be the same thickness so the growing tissue can join properly.

▶ **Best time of grafting:** It is best to avoid grafting in inclement seasons such as the winter.

▶ **Hardiness of the parts:** The graft and host must be equally hardy to avoid imbalances.

▶ **Polarity:** In the simplest terms, the buds of the graft must be grafted correctly with the tips pointing upward and not towards the ground.

There are various types of possible grafts depending on the types of plants to be grafted and the area involved. Generally speaking, there are two categories of grafts: crown grafts and base grafts. **Crown grafts** are so defined because they are done on the upper part of the host; **base grafts** are done at the base of the host plant.

This grove of conifers, with trees of different ages and a very realistic touch of moss on the trunks, is an excellent example of bonsai triangularity (see page 46).

It is important for a bonsai enthusiast to observe nature around him and to learn to recognize and understand how trees normally grow and develop in their natural environment.

Grafted plants will require attention: joints (that hold the two parts together) and the appearance of pests must be watched closely, and the plant must be watered regularly. When it is time to transplant the plant into a bonsai pot, we will cut off one third of the taproot, which is the longest root, to promote the growth of a well-developed root structure. Usually it takes a couple years before a grafted plant is able to undergo bonsai treatment.

BONSAI FOUND IN NATURE

This is a low cost method (provided the plant collection is not in violation of property rights or current laws) for obtaining excellent bonsai plants and avoiding the care required by the tech-niques described above. While walking in the woods, you may come across small plants grown from seeds that have all the characteristics of becoming excellent bonsai.

The most delicate aspect of reclaiming a plant found in nature is transplanting. In fact, a sudden change in environment is enough to compromise the success of this procedure. To insure a good chance of success, we must therefore proceed with extreme caution.

First, we must select specimens with a structure (branches, trunk, etc.) that already exhibits the characteristics that we intend to give to our bonsai. Then, we will make a visual inspection of the plant's health. Leaves must be small and uniformly distributed throughout the foliage. By contrast, roots must branch off in a circular pattern from the base of the trunk.

This is an extremely important quality in the assessment of a bonsai.

Also, bear in mind that conifers are much easier to transplant than deciduous plants.

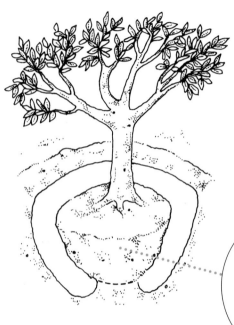

▶ Once an optimum specimen has been chosen and the surrounding area has been cleared of weeds and debris, we will dig a trough a little wider than the plant's root ball and about fifteen centimeters deep in order to remove the root structure without damaging it. Remember that the extent of root growth is normally equal to the breadth of the foliage.

▶ Working carefully, lift the plant with its soil, and wrap it in a fine net. If the place where it is to be moved is far away, wrap the root structure with moist gauze and make sure to spray the foliage with water from time to time. To keep things simple, you may also put the plant in a plastic bag that will maintain moisture without the need for time-consuming spraying.

▶ Since transplanting is, in and of itself, a highly traumatic procedure, do not put the plant directly into a small bonsai pot. Instead, initially place it in a regular flowerpot that is more suitable for accommodating the root structure, which must not be pruned under any circumstances at this time.

Once the transplant has been completed, fill empty spaces with the appropriate soil, use a support to help the plant stay erect, and water generously until water comes out of the drainage holes.

The picture shows how to properly remove a young plant found in nature without harming the root structure.

▶ Place the plant in an area protected from the wind and direct sunlight, and avoid using fertilizer for a couple of months since it could damage the root structure which is still weak.

If you have been careful, after a few months the plant will show signs of recovery and will start sending out shoots.

Remember that the ideal season for collecting a plant in nature is the spring, just before new buds appear.

Proper Repotting Techniques

We will now turn our attention to one of the "fundamental" procedures for the proper maintenance of bonsai: repotting. When you see bonsai containers, which, as you recall, come in different colors and sizes to adhere to the various styles of this art of cultivation, you will be surprised at how shallow they are (especially for group bonsai).

Thus, it is often necessary to anchor trees to the bottom of the container to keep them from moving.

▶ The most important thing is to select the proper period so the plant does not suffer excessively from the change of location and recovers rapidly. Depending on the species, the best period for repotting is from late spring and early summer to late summer and early fall.

▶ Bonsai pots have holes on the bottom that prevent water stagnation and allow roots to come in contact with oxygen. Thus, before starting the repotting procedure, it is necessary to place a wire mesh over this hole that will allow water and air to circulate, but at the same time will prevent the soil base used for repotting to escape.

Drainage holes
Whatever their appearance, all pots must have these. They allow excess water to escape, and prevent rot formation on roots.

Wire mesh
A wire mesh must be positioned over the drainage hole to prevent soil from escaping, and to make it easier to anchor the plant to the pot.

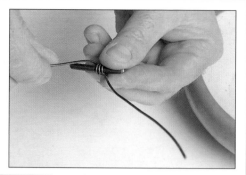

▶ The series of photographs on this page shows how to prepare metal wire and fasten it to the wire mesh on the bottom of the container. It will then be used to secure the roots and stabilize the plant. For group bonsai, wire will be used only for the larger plants, and the other specimens will be supported by these (again with wire). This

anchoring will be removed once the bonsai has developed a sufficient root structure (approximately 5-6 months from planting).

▶ Cut approximately 40 cm of the wire (the actual size will depend on the container and the distance between holes) that you will need for anchoring (with a diameter of 1-1.5 mm), and wind it around a thicker piece of wire (4-5 mm in diameter) a few centimeters long, leaving two ends of the same length.

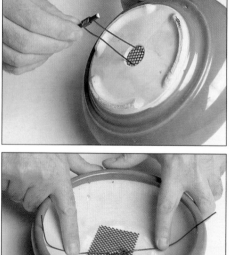

▶ From the outside, thread the wires through the holes of the wire mesh. Turn the container around and position the wire so it adheres to the bottom along the pot's diameter. At this point you may put the first layer of soil in the pot.

▶ An important and delicate phase of the repotting procedure is the cleaning and examination of the roots of the plant you are working with. In fact, it is necessary to determine which roots should be removed because they are dead or because they have grown excessively and become unmanageable (see photographs at right).

▶ Once the roots are clean, place the bonsai in its container. An oval bonsai pot was used for the specimen photographed which can then be arranged in many different ways. During this phase, for containers in other shapes, pay close attention to the "front of the bonsai" which is the side to be shown to observers.

▶ Now, very gently secure the root structure of the plant with the wire, cover with soil and water.

After anchoring, make sure that the wire is not too tight, and then eliminate any excess.

Before pruning it is necessary to take a close look at the bonsai in order to prune only where it is actually necessary.

▶ After repotting the plant in its container, look at it closely and assess its overall structure bearing in mind the style it is to be trained in. This will allow you to determine any branches to be removed (for example, a branch that "sticks out" against someone looking at the bonsai).

▶ In the three photographs at right, the branches that should be eliminated from the above plant are indicated. This will give the plant structure the triangularity that is one of the basic principals of bonsai cultivation.

▶ After pruning, apply a wound sealing mastic to the larger branch incisions to limit the escape of sap and reduce the likelihood of infestation by fungi and pests.

PRUNING TIPS

Always proceed carefully supporting the branches you are working on as necessary to avoid breaking them. The tool used, clippers or scissors, must be sharp and carefully disinfected before using. This will help to prevent tissue death and the development of infections.

The lowest branch needs to grow. Therefore, don't prune it.

PRUNING BONSAI

We have described bonsai as miniature trees. As exceptional plants, they require special care. Pruning is one of the fundamental procedures for obtaining bonsai worthy of that name.

This procedure is performed using small, sharp scissors that are able to easily penetrate the intricate vegetation of the foliage and remove unwanted branches and buds with precision.

Pruning should be repeated periodically to control the development of the bonsai. A branch that has a tendency to grow too fast should be partially cut, or buds at the tip should be removed. After this procedure, the branch will develop minor branches that will grow in width to form full and harmonious foliage. Technically this type of pruning is called "cutting back" and follows different principles depending on the shape to be given to the bonsai (*moyogi, chokkan, kengai,* etc.) and the plant species to be raised (pines, spruce firs, maples, ginkgo, etc.). However, there are two distinct techniques that are common to all styles

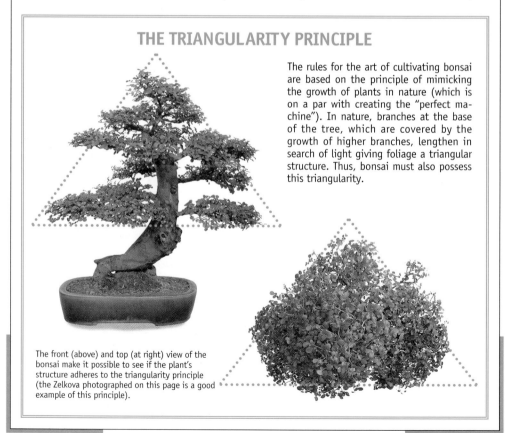

THE TRIANGULARITY PRINCIPLE

The rules for the art of cultivating bonsai are based on the principle of mimicking the growth of plants in nature (which is on a par with creating the "perfect machine"). In nature, branches at the base of the tree, which are covered by the growth of higher branches, lengthen in search of light giving foliage a triangular structure. Thus, bonsai must also possess this triangularity.

The front (above) and top (at right) view of the bonsai make it possible to see if the plant's structure adheres to the triangularity principle (the Zelkova photographed on this page is a good example of this principle).

and species: branch pruning and shoot and leaf pruning.

BRANCH PRUNING

In the appropriate tables at the end of the book, we will see how to prune branches based on the style or species raised. Below are some fundamental rules that apply in all cases.

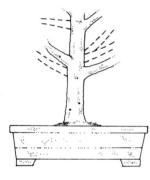

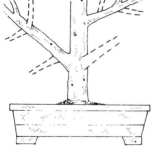

In the drawings, the branches shown with dotted lines should be pruned since they have no purpose, regardless of the bonsai style desired.

▶ In contrast to plants raised to produce fruit or wood, the purpose of bonsai is essentially aesthetic. Thus, pruning will be used to do away with branches that are of no interest from the standpoint of the person viewing the bonsai such as those that grow towards the vantage point of the onlooker.

▶ Again, for aesthetic reasons, the branches growing at the base of the trunk up to about one third of the trunk's height should be eliminated.

▶ As in the case of unsightly branches, sick branches should also be removed completely.

▶ When pruning, do not trim branches to the same size. Instead, make them different lengths leaving each one the vital space to develop harmoniously.

▶ When cutting a branch, smooth the surface of the cut well and try to get as close to the trunk as possible. Ideally, you should use shears with curved blades to allow the bark to cover the wound as it grows.

PRUNING
A POMEGRANATE

The foliage of this specimen of pomegranate has a few branches that cross each other, which, in the practice of bonsai, is considered a mistake. Exceptions to this rule are those cases in which it is necessary to close a space left open by a dead branch, or to reestablish a missing portion of foliage that is considered essential. In these cases, branches are allowed to grow "out of place," and they must be trained on the basis of requirements. To properly maintain the shape of the bonsai illustrated on these pages, it is necessary to prune in the spring. However, this will mean foregoing the marvelous flowering and subsequent fruiting that is typical of this species.

Pruning during the growth season often means sacrificing flowering and fruiting.

49

PRUNING AN *ELEAGNUS*

The *eleagnus* illustrated on this page was recently potted, and it still cannot properly be called a "bonsai." The left branch will be used to establish the top of the plant to correct the lack of triangularity and depth.

After pruning

Leaves
When pruned properly, plants are able to produce new small branches with a greater number of smaller leaves.

Branch
This small branch is used to give triangularity to the foliage.

Determine which is the main branch, or "leading branch." This is especially important since it is used to establish the final shape of the plant.

After pruning

PRUNING A *CARMONA*

In this case we are also pruning a pre-bonsai plant, i.e., a young plant that has just been potted. This *carmona macrophilla*, also called a tea plant, will undergo a radical transformation. An attempt will be made to convert it from an upside-down broom style to an informal upright style.

Thus, all branches that do not serve this purpose must be eliminated, and with a great deal of time and patience, we will try to shape the new structure by identifying layers and the top.

Shaping the top
will require patience and precision since this is an essential and aesthetically important part of the plant.

Unwanted branches
This branch may be eliminated or skillfully shaped. For now, let the plant develop, and prune at a later time.

Main branch
After identifying this branch, it must be allowed to grow and thicken since it will be instrumental in the aesthetic equilibrium of the bonsai.

HOW TO DIRECT A BRANCH UPWARD

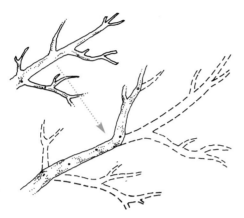

When a branch of a small plant, which is to be raised as a bonsai, does not go where it is "supposed to," it is possible to correct growth with the appropriate pruning procedure. Before doing so, look at it closely, and determine the correct spot for making the cut in order to obtain the desired effect (see drawing). Always remember to cover the wounds with wound paste, and monitor the growth of the branch eliminating any downward facing buds.

▶ For bonsai, most pruning should be done during the growing period when the plant is at the height of developing vegetation. This will give you a more precise idea of the cuts to make based on the results desired.

▶ Bonsai in their golden years are held in great esteem. With appropriate pruning, it is possible to increase the lifeline of the plant we are cultivating.
In this respect, we repeat that the largest branches in an adult tree are on the lower part of the trunk, while smaller branches are at the top.

▶ Deciduous trees (maples, elms, etc.) need frequent attention since instead of growing taller, pruned branches divide in-

The elimination of a specific branch, for example, can be motivated by the fact that it prevents the foliage from taking a cone shape.

HOW TO DIRECT A BRANCH DOWNWARD

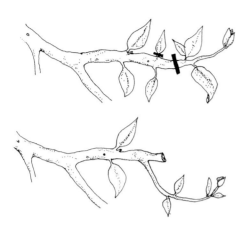

It is also possible to use pruning if you want to direct the growth of a branch downward.

In bonsai plants, this is a rather frequent requirement. In fact, when observed, the tiny plant should not look flat, but should convey a three-dimensional quality. Therefore, it must have a certain amount of depth. Directing branches downward may turn out to be a particularly useful trick for the bonsai enthusiast.

Remember, before making cuts, it is always necessary to look closely at the plant we are working on, in an attempt to anticipate the outcome of our procedure (see drawing above). A true branch cut is, indeed, a very quick and easy procedure, but we should never forget that it takes nature months, if not years, to correct our mistakes.

In general, branches should be cut at the base, but it is also necessary to be careful with those species (e.g., maples) that have so-called "running sap" that could have an adverse effect on the good health of the plant.

In this case it is necessary to leave a spike a few millimeters in size that will be removed once it is obvious the sap has dried up. Always carefully disinfect the wound with a wound sealing mastic.

The success of our efforts can be confirmed only in the spring when new leaves sprout.

to a multitude of small branches that give shape and thickness to the foliage.

▶ If you want to weaken a branch, it is enough to trim it by removing the end. By contrast, a branch left undisturbed will get stronger.

▶ Before pruning deciduous plants, it would be a good idea to let the branches forming the shape of the tree to grow undisturbed for at least a couple years so they can develop adequately.

▶ When a particularly thick branch is being pruned, it is wise to disinfect the wound with an appropriate antifungal or wound sealing product.

For branch and leaf pruning procedures, it is always important to use the right tool for the job.
Thus, don't be misled by sales pitches.
The tools actually needed by a bonsai enthusiast can be counted on your fingers.

PRUNING SUPERIMPOSED BRANCHES

The growth of superimposed branches is a defect frequently found in so-called "pre-bonsai" plants (young plants that have just been potted, and that are starting to be given a style direction), but sometimes also in those already considered to be "bonsai." These are two branches that are rather close to each other growing on top and parallel to each other creating an undesirable aesthetic effect based on criteria used in the art of bonsai that have been cited frequently.

After selecting which of the two branches to keep (based on an assessment of the plant's structure, cone shape and intended style), the unwanted branch is cut off using pruning shears with curved blades. Thanks to this tool, the cut will fill in more easily with a partial covering of bark giving the plant a particularly realistic appearance.

HOW TO PRUNE BRANCHES THAT CROSS

Crossing branches in bonsai are considered a defect. This can occur as a result of the natural inclination the plant assumes with growth, or because maintenance pruning is done at the incorrect time or in the wrong manner.

In the example illustrated, the branch is growing towards the center creating obvious disharmony. After selecting the exact spot to prune, the appropriate scissors should be used.

Immediately after pruning, it is clear that the structure has improved and become lighter.

Don't forget to treat the area of the cut with a wound sealing mastic.

PRUNING SHOOTS AND LEAVES

While branch pruning serves primarily to establish the basic shape of the bonsai, shoot and leaf pruning makes it possible to refine and improve the shape aesthetically. Below are several basic rules for removing shoots and leaves properly.

▶ The frequency of trimming shoots depends on the type of tree raised. For further information, see the table at the end of the book.

▶ The period for performing this type of pruning varies from the spring to the fall depending on the type of plant (again, see the tables at the end of the book).

▶ Frequent pruning of shoots on deciduous trees will generate foliage made up of smaller leaves that produce an overall gracious effect.

▶ In conifers, shoot trimming is called pinching. In addition to maintaining the plant's shape, it encourages the growth of small needles.

▶ For bonsai with beautiful flowering, shoots should be removed once flowers have withered.

▶ Pruning shoots stimulates the growth of others. We should attempt to favor this type of pruning when required by the bonsai (e.g., to fill in a bare spot).

▶ On conifers, pinching is done with the fingers. On other plants it is usual-

All bonsai enthusiasts must have a leaf remover for making a cut that is both clean and delicate.

DEFOLIATION PRUNING

Defoliation is a procedure performed on certain varieties of deciduous trees which results in an increased number of smaller leaves. This is done by removing almost all the plant's vegetation, leaving only 1-2 small leaves on each branch, thereby encouraging the tree to produce new foliage.

Defoliation is usually done in June and July, and only on plants in good health. Also pay close attention to watering: plants without foliage are susceptible to insufficient or excessive watering.

The drawing shows the result of pinching back a conifer shoot.

A problem common to all conifers, which are generally large and robust plants, is that their long needles do not suit the small size of the bonsai (the photograph shows a pinus nigra *[Austrian black pine]). In addition to keeping the plant in full sun and properly watered, pinch back its shoots as shown in the drawing.*

ly done using the appropriate leaf-removing tool.

DEFOLIATION TECHNIQUE

Defoliation, or the removal of all the leaves on a branch, is a radical pruning technique making it possible to develop two years' worth of vegetation in one season. This should be done during the plant's growth phase, between May and July. Leaves should be cut with a clean pair of scissors leaving only leaf stems on the branch, or at most, a quarter of the leaf.

At the base of leaf stems, the plant will soon produce new leaves of a smaller size producing a pleasing aesthetic effect. This procedure should only be performed on plants in excellent health. Remember that leaves of deciduous plants should be thinned out from time to time to prevent the formation of unsightly leaf clumps.

THICKENING
THE TRUNK AND BRANCHES

When you have a bonsai with a trunk that is too slender for the foliage – and this happens frequently – you can increase its size and restore its proportions. To do this, in the spring wrap a piece of aluminum wire around the base of the plant to produce a choking effect that will gradually make the trunk bigger. In the fall of the same year, remove the wire to prevent damage to the plant. The wire should be applied correctly: not too tight or too loose. If too tight, it could cut off the sap vessels causing the plant to die. If too loose, the desired effect will not be achieved. By contrast, branches that are too thin will get larger if they are not pruned. Thus, do not prune until they have reached the desired size.

Cutting
Back Conifer Shoots

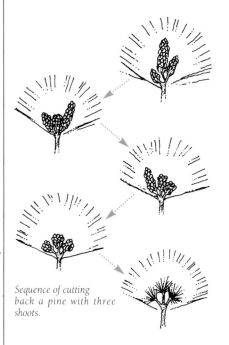

Sequence of cutting back a pine with three shoots.

Pruning conifer shoots, which is also called pinching, can be done with your hands. New shoots that, fully grown, could compromise the structure of the plant, should be removed from various branches delicately and with forethought. This forces the plant to form buds (even on areas of old wood), and consequently, to grow new branches. A few bunches of needles must be left so the small branches will not dry out. Any pruning done during the growth season will cause new shoots to appear near the pruning site. Thus, this is the most effective way to fill in bare spots.

Sequence of cutting back a pine with two shoots.

Pinching may be used on pines, junipers and many other conifers.

How to Thicken a Trunk Correctly

There are bonsai that have a good structure and pleasing foliage, but have a base that is inadequate, not cone shaped, and not up to the quality of the rest of the plant. In these cases binding can be used as indicated in the series of photographs on this page for a ficus bonsai.

It may appear to be a simple procedure, but it should be done carefully and attentively. It is important to work close to the ground just above the point of attachment of the roots to avoid unsightly results. The wire should not be too tight, or the sap vessels will be harmed causing the plant to die.

Above: Good results obtained from binding the trunk of this ficus are obvious. The base is clearly larger than before.

The Jinning Technique

Jinning is a bonsai technique that consists of chopping off the end of a branch with the appropriate tool (*jinning* clippers or special cutters) and removing the remaining bark attached to the trunk.

This technique, which is very effective on conifers, is used to achieve particular evocative effects since it recreates a classic trunk appearance caused by a bolt of lightning or other natural calamity. As a result, the bonsai takes on a "lifelike" appearance, and as we know, this is a desired quality for bonsai. Because it is difficult to use *jinning* clippers properly, they

Stages of work to create the jinning effect (above and at left) and the shari *effect (below).*

should only be used by skillful bonsai enthusiasts.

After creating the *jinning* effect, spread a bleach solution (generally barium polysulfide) on the area to prevent the dead wood from rotting, and to contribute to the "aging" of the area worked. This technique can also be used to create the *shari* effect, which consists of the furrowing of the trunk to simulate the effect of corrosion.

These techniques should only be applied to bonsai with the proper shape (simulating trees in the high mountains, for instance), or there is a risk of irreparably damaging the appearance of the plant.

Using the jinning technique can give the bonsai a slimmer and more balanced appearance, and makes it possible to realistically simulate the effects of the passage of time.

The most appropriate plants for the jinning technique are conifers since they have resinous and dense wood.

A juniperus chinensis that is approximately 70 years old in the informal upright style.

When using the shari technique, it is necessary to carefully follow the pattern of sap vessels to avoid compromising the health of the bonsai.

Pinus pentaphylla
trained in the informal upright style. The layering of branches is good.

Foliage
Thanks to proper pinching, good layer coverage has been achieved.

Trunk
Bearing witness to the age of the bonsai, the trunk is one of its most important parts.

Layers
To display the structure more effectively, pruning must be consistent.

USING WIRE

Wire can be used whenever you want to change the slant of a branch or trunk to comply with a particular bonsai shape. For this procedure, copper or aluminum wire should be used (other metals are not suitable), which should be purchased in different diameters to meet varying needs.

▶ Wire should be wound at an angle of 45° to the trunk line, and the length of the wire should be double the length of the branch you wish to correct.

The diameter of the wire to be used for binding should be selected as a function of the size of the branches you wish to bind.

It should be noted that certain plants with soft bark, such as maples, apricot trees and thorn bushes in general, may suffer from direct contact with bare wire.

▶ In determining proper wire diameter, it should be approximately one third the diameter of the branch to be corrected.

▶ Wire should be applied by wrapping it around the part in question in a regular spiral pattern taking care not to overlap or cross the wire which could be damaging or unsightly.

▶ Once the procedure is completed, the loose end of the wire should be doubled over so it will not cause injuries during bonsai maintenance.

To perform binding properly, hold the branch you wish to bend with your left hand, and wrap the wire around the branch in a spiral pattern with your right hand.
In this manner you will avoid breaking or damaging the branch.

On the opposite page above:
How to properly shape a branch.

▶ If you wish to reinforce the binding effect, it is sufficient to join two wires of the same diameter, which should be kept parallel when binding.

▶ Remember not to apply wire when new vegetation is coming out because the plant, which is full of sap, would not withstand the constriction (for the right time to apply wire, see the tables at the end of the book).

▶ The length of time the wire must remain in place depends on the specimen. In general, this is from 6 to 8 months for deciduous plants, and from 12 to 18 months for conifers. Bear in mind that this information is for indicative purposes only and could change

Before binding, the direction of this branch should be changed to give foliage greater depth.

PROPER BINDING PROCEDURES

Before starting to bind the branch you wish to train, it is first necessary to anchor the wire around the trunk. Working carefully, wrap the wire on the branch, and then shape it in the direction desired.

substantially from specimen to specimen and from style to style.

Thus, monitor the outcome of the procedure constantly making sure that the wire does not start to make notches in the wood. The application of wire involves an enormous sacrifice and expenditure of energy on the part of the plant undergoing the procedure. Accordingly, if you do not achieve the desired results after the application period, do not repeat the procedure immediately. Instead, let the bonsai rest for a period of 6 – 7 months.

▶ Binding should not be too tight or too loose.

▶ A rule of thumb is that wire should never be applied to bonsai that, during

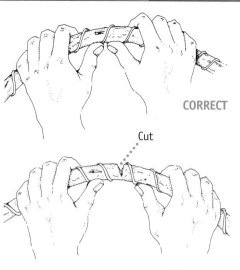

CORRECT

Cut

INCORRECT

The wire must be left in position until the branch assumes the desired direction. This period should not be excessive or, as the plant grows, the wire will tend to leave an indelible mark on the bark of the plant or it may even remain "fused" to the branch making it nearly impossible to remove.

Drawing above:
The branch should be manipulated carefully and firmly in order to bend it without running the risk of breaking it.

After binding the structure of the plant is more harmonious.

the current year, were or will be repotted. In fact, it would be difficult for the plant to withstand two closely occurring procedures that require such an enormous expenditure of energy.

▶ Finally, when bending branches, do so carefully using the thumbs as a support when shaping.

The drawings depict the change in structure of a pine as a result of binding.

Using a young specimen, but one that has a good cone shape, it is possible to transform it into an "ancient" bonsai by properly binding branches (and also through the sensible use of pruning).

WHAT TO DO AFTER BINDING

Once the binding is complete, let the bonsai rest in a shaded area protected from drafts, and make sure to give it a good watering.

The wire used to shape the branch must be removed at the precise moment when it could potentially strangle the plant. If all goes well, the wire is usually removed in the fall before the dormant period. To do this, cut the wire into several segments with the appropriate cutters to avoid causing shock or damage to the bonsai. In the inauspicious event that the wire has made a notch in, and penetrated the bark, it will be necessary to unwind the wire delicately and disinfect the wound with appropriate healing agents.

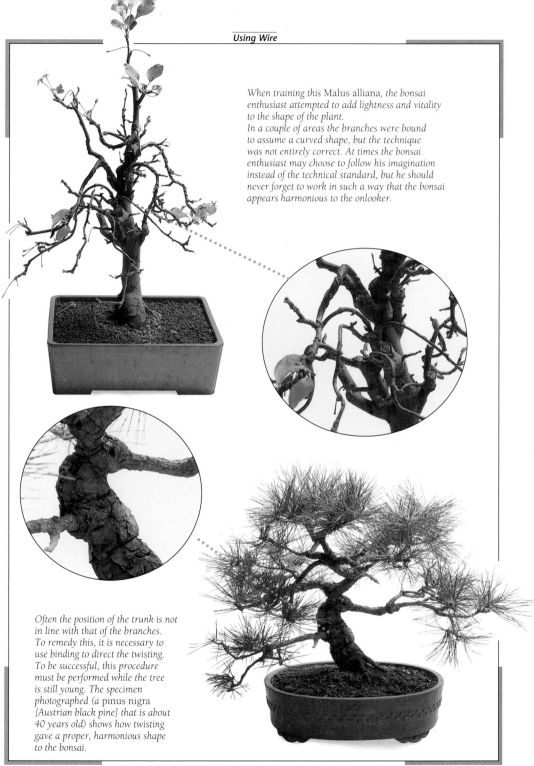

When training this Malus alliana, *the bonsai enthusiast attempted to add lightness and vitality to the shape of the plant.*
In a couple of areas the branches were bound to assume a curved shape, but the technique was not entirely correct. At times the bonsai enthusiast may choose to follow his imagination instead of the technical standard, but he should never forget to work in such a way that the bonsai appears harmonious to the onlooker.

Often the position of the trunk is not in line with that of the branches. To remedy this, it is necessary to use binding to direct the twisting. To be successful, this procedure must be performed while the tree is still young. The specimen photographed (a pinus nigra [Austrian black pine] that is about 40 years old) shows how twisting gave a proper, harmonious shape to the bonsai.

OTHER TECHNIQUES
FOR CORRECTING BRANCHES

In addition to pruning and wire binding, there are many other techniques to change the shape of a bonsai branch or tree.

Noteworthy among these are: the lowering of branches using braces anchored to the tray (1); the separation of two branches that are too close with small pieces of wood (2); the lowering of a branch by hanging small weights on it (3); and the straightening of curved branches using clamps (4 and 5).

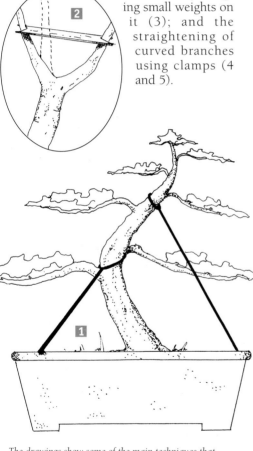

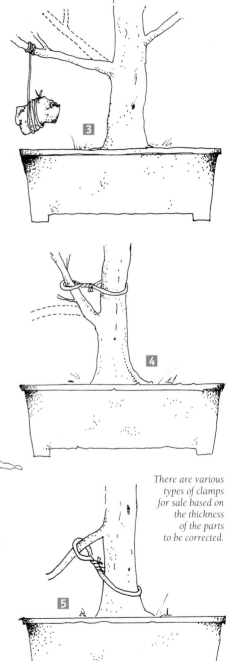

There are various types of clamps for sale based on the thickness of the parts to be corrected.

The drawings show some of the main techniques that can be used to correct the direction of bonsai branches and trunks. However, the technique in figure 1, the application of braces anchored to the tray, can only be used on very young specimens.

REPOTTING

Repotting is an extremely delicate procedure that should be repeated several times during the life of the bonsai. Accordingly, it should be done with great precision keeping in mind all applicable rules of plant and soil sciences.

▶ The best time for repotting is the **spring** when plants come back to life. This will allow the bonsai to rapidly recover from the shock resulting from this procedure.

▶ It is up to you to decide whether to repot a bonsai or not based on an assessment of the plant's needs and aesthetic factors. The rules followed for ordinary decorative plants do not apply to the repotting of bonsai. In other words, a small pot is not merely replaced by a larger pot to provide greater space for the growing root structure. This, in fact, would be contrary to the goal of our art. With regard to bonsai, on the other hand, the aim is to remove the plant to **reduce the size of the root structure** in order to encourage the growth of new root hairs. Although the latter are compressed into a small space, they are the main means of absorption, and thus, they are responsible for providing nutrition to the plant. The bonsai may be returned to the same pot, or put in a pot with a different shape, but with the same size as the old pot.

PREPARING THE CONTAINER

In addition to meeting shape and size requirements, the container used to hold the bonsai must be clean and sterilized to kill germs and pests. The bottom must have one or more drainage holes covered with a fine plastic wire mesh to allow water to drain easily while preventing the escape of soil. In low containers, the roots will be secured to this wire mesh using copper wire binding to give greater stability to the bonsai (see pages 41-43).

Small plants that we select at a nursery must have a good structure, even if young.

1

2

3

4

HOW TO REPOT

If you have to transfer a bonsai from one container to another, or remove it to prune the root structure, it is important to work with dry soil. This will make it easier for you to separate the plant from its old container and will facilitate work with the roots.

When removing the bonsai from the old container, never grab it by the trunk. This could cause a large number of root hairs to break. Instead, remove it by turning the pot upside down and tapping the bottom lightly to dislodge the contents.

▶ Separate the root structure from the soil by carefully using a stick, and prune any roots that are unruly or too long by a third of their length using sharp and clean tools.

REPOTTING TOOLS

Repotting is always a delicate time for bonsai. It should be done at the most appropriate time to insure an excellent recovery for the plant, and the specimens to be repotted must be in perfect health. It is also important to use the most suitable tools to make the procedure as painless as possible.

The **pot** (1) must be specifically designed for bonsai and constructed using special techniques that allow it to withstand changes in temperature. The **wire mesh** (2), which may be plastic or metal, is necessary to cover the drainage hole. **Sifters** (3) are used to make uniform the soil structure used, and the **rake** (4) is used to arrange the soil properly.

to facilitate the elimination of air pockets that could damage the root structure.

▶ When finished with this procedure, the only thing left to do is to give the plant a good watering with a mister, a watering can with a sprinkling attachment, or by immersing the pot in water up to the brim.

▶ Afterwards, situate the plant in a shady area that is protected from the wind for about twenty days. The first fertilizer treatment should occur no earlier than a couple months after repotting.

One part of the art of bonsai is dedicated to the crafting of special containers that are often in unusual shapes and decorated with oriental motifs.

Eliminate broken or dead roots, and if necessary, trim the taproot, which is the largest main root of the root structure.

▶ Once you have completed pruning, put the plant back in the pot, and, using a stick, arrange the roots on the first layer of soil making sure the plant is in the correct position. In fact, this is extremely important for both the aesthetic appeal of the bonsai and the proper depth relationship between soil and roots. The latter must not be too low or too high above the surface level.

Among the tools that all bonsai enthusiasts must have are cutters with straight blades for removing the hardiest branches, and root scissors. Always keep them sharpened so cuts will be clean.

▶ After examining the plant, add more soil, but avoid filling the container to the brim, and press down the sold very lightly

71

Repotting

The sequence of photographs on these pages shows, step by step, how to repot a bonsai correctly.

Before beginning, it is first important to determine the actual need for repotting. This is usually indicated by an excessive number of roots that start to appear on the surface near the edges of the container since they have run out of room to spread out in the pot's soil base.

After cutting the wire that anchored the root ball to the old vase, the roots should be examined to determine their distribution, and it should be noted whether they are healthy, and whether there is a sufficient

Please note: The need for repotting is indicated by roots protruding out of the drainage holes and over the edges of the container.

This enlargement makes it possible to see the rootlets attached to the root. These anchor the plant to the soil and absorb water and nutrients. Since rootlets are very delicate, handle the bonsai's root structure with care.

or excessive number of them.

Using a stick, very carefully separate the roots from the soil leaving them completely clean. If this is a difficult procedure, rather than risk damaging the root structure, it is better to immerse the bonsai in a container of water (to which you have added an appropriate disinfectant to insure roots are not attacked by rot or fungi).

Using scissors, start pruning the roots that have been fully cleaned. First prune the tap root. It may be reduced substantially in size only if there are sufficient roots at the base of the tree to assure the plant's survival. Dead or damaged areas should be removed, and the root ball should be reduced by up to a third (but only on plants in perfect health such as the specimen in the photograph). Remember that capillaries, the smallest of all roots, are those that supply nutrients.

When you have completed pruning, position the plant in the new container as indicated in the sequence of photographs on pages 41-43.

When repotting is completed, it is also necessary to prune the foliage of the bonsai. In fact, it must be reduced to the same degree that the roots were pruned. This technique will make it easier for the bonsai to withstand the trauma of repotting. Remember that after this procedure, it is likely the plant will lose a few leaves.

After pruning
After a while, this branch may be bound to give greater depth to the foliage.

The foliage
of the repotted bonsai must be reduced in proportion to the percentage of roots removed.

Correction of branches
If this procedure is necessary, do it some time after repotting so as not to put the bonsai under additional stress.

Pruning
Remember also to prune those branches growing in the direction of the onlooker (the front of the bonsai) and to reduce leaf surface by eliminating the largest and least harmonious leaves.

This pomegranate (trained in the slanted style), which is characterized by areas of dry wood hardened by time, conveys to the onlooker the plant's desire to live. After a few more years of work (skillful pruning and binding), its structure will be more harmonious.

This is a ficus panda shaped in the semi-cascade style in a delicately decorated pot. With proper maintenance pruning, it will be possible to slim the form of the bonsai and show the layers that are now partially hidden by foliage.

PLANT CARE

THE SOIL

The main qualities for good bonsai soil are pliability, the right balance of components, and water capacity, meaning the ability to absorb water and to allow water to drain.

▶ Several components contribute to the **soil structure** for bonsai. These are mixed in differing proportions based on the type of plant they must feed, and choices made by the bonsai enthusiast. One of the most widely used mixes calls for equal parts of rich garden soil, forest soil or peat, and sterile river sand. Rich soil makes up the base of the mixture; forest soil and peat contribute humus, a substance that is fundamental for the life of plants; and sand gives the mix the necessary pliability to promote the circulation of air and drainage of water.

SOIL TYPES

The various types of soil base available for sale meet the many potential needs of plants.

Sand (1): Indispensable for maintaining the correct level of moisture and facilitating root formation.
Fine akadama clay (2): Volcanic soil for species requiring basic pH.
Kanuma clay (3): Volcanic soil for species requiring acidic soil.
Pozzuolana (4) Useful for proper soil drainage.
Conifer soil (5): Suitable for all species requiring well-drained soils that are slightly acidic.
Gravel (6): Necessary for proper drainage of the soil base.
Coarse Akadama clay (7): In conjunction with fine akadama clay, provides the makings for soil with excellent structure.

Allowing the structure to grow
in certain areas makes it possible, over time,
to achieve a good conical shape that improves
the style (informal upright style).

**The depth of the
container should be**
roughly equal to the width
of the base of the trunk.
Thus, this Cotoneaster was
put in a pot that is too
deep. However, certain
species (especially young
plants) may need deep
containers to produce fruit.

**Containers
that are too big
or too deep**
for the plants they
hold are one of the
most prevalent
defects of bonsai
that are purchased.

▶ With regard to moisture, bonsai require **constant**, but not excessive, **moisture**. This is the reason why sand and a layer of fine gravel are usually put on the bottom of the container before distributing the bonsai soil mix.

Broadleaf and young trees that grow rapidly prefer a base soil mix with a low percentage of rich soil, while conifers, slow-growing plants and old plants require a higher percentage of sand. Thus, a good mix for broadleaf plants would be made up of one part forest soil, one part peat, and one part sand. An equally excellent mix for conifers should contain one part rich soil, one part peat and two parts sand. Anyone who is not adept at making this mix should feel free to select a universal soil mix that can be purchased at specialized stores.

A good specimen of Murraya paniculata *(orange jessamine) trained in the formal upright style and perfectly positioned in an old Chinese pot. The specimen needs pruning to fully accentuate the style and form. Of particular interest in this species is the abundant flowering with an intoxicating scent that later gives way to red berries.*

▶ Special attention must be focused on pH, the degree of acidity in our mix. In fact, to grow well, each plant requires a certain degree of acidity that can be measured with a relatively inexpensive device called a pH meter.

If the pH of the mix does not match the pH requirement of the plant being cultivated, we can correct it by balancing the components of the mix, or by adding special substances called soil correctives.

Thus, if a plant, such as an azalea, needs highly acidic soil, we will put more peat in our mixture which is more acidic by nature. If, on the other hand, a plant, such as an apple tree, requires soil with low acidity, we will add only a small amount of peat, and may further correct it by adding small amounts of lime or calcium carbonate.

However, most bonsai plants require soil with pH values ranging between 5.5 and 6, which are satisfied by universal soil.

▶ Once the dry mix has been prepared, it should be poured through a sieve with a 0.5 mm mesh in order to eliminate all large particles that could impair the plant's nutrition process.

The mix should then be spread evenly over the layer of gravel on the bottom of the container up to 3 cm from the edge of the container.

The level will be topped off (at approximately 1 cm from the edge) with the addition of ground dry moss or a fine mixture composed of leaf mulch, rich soil, sand and peat.

When preparing the new plant bed, do not put any type of fertilizer in the ground since at this stage it could be harmful to the plant's roots.

This Zelkova nire with a powerful trunk, was positioned in a container with the proper shape.

To achieve the proper triangularity of the structure, it is necessary to make this branch grow.

FERTILIZING

The nutritional elements included in soil are not sufficient by themselves to satisfy all the needs of a bonsai. In addition, the delicate procedures performed on the plant – repotting, pruning, wire binding, etc. – require the plant to use energy that is only partially recovered from the soil it lives in. Thus, it is necessary to use a balanced fertilizer that contains all nutritional elements necessary for the plant to live.

▶ Plants should be fertilized any time during the growing season, generally from March to October. Initially, it is sufficient to fertilize once every 20 days, but in the fall, fertilizer should be applied weekly to better prepare the small tree for the dormant period ahead.

WATERING AIDS

Watering is an important procedure for maintaining bonsai, and accordingly the right equipment must be used. A watering can (1) and mister (2) can be used to meet most of the plant's needs. In particular, the mister is useful for sprinkling leaves when the plant needs moisture and for applying pesticides.

The wire mesh (3) allows excess water to escape from container holes. The spatula end of the rake (4) can be used to check moisture in low areas of the soil base. Sifters (5) and scoops (6) can be used for working the soil base depending on specific requirements.

▶ Fertilizer should be applied to conifers (spruce, pines) starting in February since their growing season starts before that of deciduous trees. For the latter, fertilizing should be stopped from October to March, i.e., during the dormant period, to avoid damage to the root structure.

▶ Keep in mind that solid fertilizers provide their main nutrients to the soil more slowly than liquid products. In addition to nitrogen-based fertilizers, we suggest using organic fertilizers that are particu-larly rich in microelements. Excellent results are also obtained using fertilizers with an ox blood base.

WATERING

Normal plants are able to meet their need for water by reaching water in the soil through a deep root structure. This is not possible for small bonsai plants that must be given the necessary amount of water daily.

> Due to the meager amount of soil available to bonsai roots, watering is an extremely delicate procedure that must be repeated frequently and carefully. Failure to water could be fatal.

Water may be provided by surface sprinkling (the stream of water should not be too forceful) or by immersing the pot in water. The important thing is to make sure the plant has the necessary water balance.

In fact, the needs of a bonsai vary on the basis of its natural and vegetative condition. Following are general tips for proper watering.

▶ In the **summer** when the plant is outside, watering should be done once or twice a day during cool periods (early morning or late evening) after checking soil moisture.

▶ In the **fall**, the bonsai may initially have needs similar to those in the summer. Subsequently, it will have lower watering requirements. It will be sufficient to check soil moisture to determine when to water.

WORK TOOLS

This is a sample of the basic tools that all bonsai enthusiasts should have: branch scissors (1); scissors for small branches (2); knife-saw (3); wire brush for cleaning bark (4); tweezers and spatula (5); clamp for shaping branches or the trunk (6); jinning clippers (7); leaf removing shears (8); root scissors (9); pruning sheers with straight blades (10) for large branches; pruning sheers with curved blades (11) for cutting branches; round-head pruning sheers (12) for the total removal of branches; and wire cutters (13). When making the initial purchase of bonsai tools, it is best to lean towards high-quality tools even though this will frequently require a significant expenditure. In addition to making work easier, these tools will definitely last longer than other products offered at lower prices. Always keep cutting tools well sharpened and disinfected.

▶ In the **winter**, during the dormant period, most bonsai will need to be watered twice a week during the warmest time of the day.

▶ In the **spring**, when the growth season begins, water should be given based on the plant's condition, and watering should be more frequent as the temperature rises.

► **Deciduous trees** require more water in the summer since the greater leaf area facilitates transpiration. By contrast, **conifers** need little water, even in the winter, since they maintain their leaves even when the weather is bad.

► Although it is true that plants need water to live, remember that **excess water** can be even **more dangerous** than too little.

► Feel the soil in the pot to make sure that water being provided is also reaching the bottom of the pot. Stop watering when water comes out of the drainage holes.

For this Sigyzium with a slender structure in the formal upright style, it is best to lean towards an oval pot with a very low edge, or at the very least, a pot with rounded corners.

TOOLS

Tools used for bonsai techniques are not much different than those normally used for gardening with the exception of two tools patented by Japanese bonsai masters. The first of these, clippers with curved blades, is truly an indispensable tool for bonsai techniques. This tool allows the removal of branches leaving a slightly rounded area at the point of removal. As the wound heals, the concave area is covered by new bark, and the unsightly effects of pruning are eliminated. Using the second tool, jinning clippers, it is possible to achieve special effects when working on the bark. Because it is difficult to work with, this tool should only be used by experts.

The remaining tools are those used in day-to-day gardening:
- Wide, strong scissors for cutting roots;
- Small strong scissors for proper cutting of branches and minor branches;
- Scissors for removing shoots;
- Wire cutters for removing wire, binding and unbinding;
- Small rake with brush for repotting;
- Tweezers for the removal of dead leaves, foreign objects and dead matter;
- A pointed stick for cleaning roots;
- A small broom for cleaning;
- A small table or other convenient support.

After using a tool, to avoid rusting be sure to remove all remaining dirt from it thoroughly before putting it away.

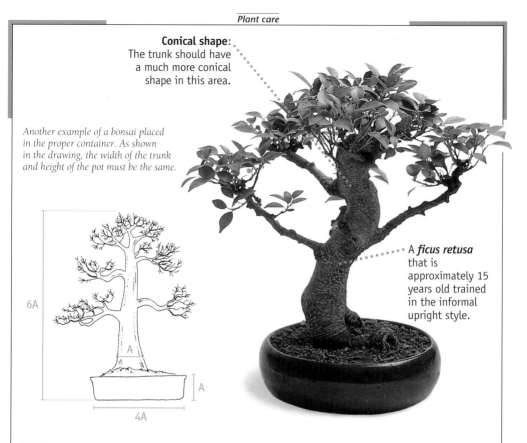

Conical shape:
The trunk should have a much more conical shape in this area.

Another example of a bonsai placed in the proper container. As shown in the drawing, the width of the trunk and height of the pot must be the same.

6A

A

A

4A

A *ficus retusa* that is approximately 15 years old trained in the informal upright style.

Disinfecting tools *is a healthy practice recommended to avoid the spread of infections. You can use a solution of copper sulfate or other disinfectant that can easily be found in stores.*

Contact a store of your choice for sharpening cutting tools.

BONSAI CONTAINERS

Up until now we have talked about growing small bonsai plants, but have left out the other aspect that is unique to bonsai - containers (often called "trays" for being so shallow), which are a fundamental aesthetic element.

The Japanese and Chinese created magnificent pots for their bonsai, and those that survived the ravages of time are invaluable pieces of art. We will be satisfied with much less, but will adhere to the very specific rules on shape, depth and color of the vase to be matched up with the plant we have raised.

In fact, each bonsai style requires the proper representation of these elements without which the work of many years would be in vain. Indeed, there are times when a bonsai, which is not particularly beautiful, makes a good impression if placed in a container that emphasizes its strong points and conceals its defects.

Bonsai containers can be purchased at special stores, but there are bonsai enthusiasts who make these pots out of clay.

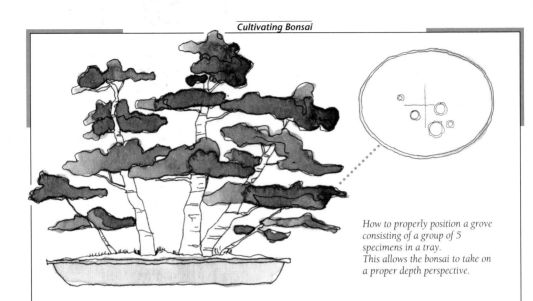

How to properly position a grove consisting of a group of 5 specimens in a tray.
This allows the bonsai to take on a proper depth perspective.

Whether pots are purchased or made, the length of the container must be two-thirds the height of the bonsai.

For plants with highly developed foliage, the length of the pot must two-thirds the size of the foliage. The depth must be equal to the diameter of the trunk, while the height of the bonsai should be approximately six times the depth of the container.

The position of the bonsai in the container is equally important to insure the full appreciation of onlookers. Accordingly, a single bonsai should not be positioned in the middle of the container, but slightly to the right or left of center. For group bonsai, your good taste should guide your placement decision.

How to place 3 specimens with differing ages and sizes in a container and obtain a realistic effect.

COLORS AND SHAPES

Pots must be porcelain or terracotta, and the inside must not be glazed in order to allow the pot to breathe and to facilitate the dispersion of any excess water.

The color and shape of containers should be matched to the type of plant raised and the bonsai style followed. Dark colors are suitable for most situations, and especially for conifer needles. Conifers look particularly good in rectangular trays. A tree with showy white flowering will stand out beautifully in a container glazed with bright colors, while a tree with red fruit will provide a pleasant contrast in a darkly colored container.

Oval trays are particularly well suited for the upside-down broom style. Trays of the same shape, but a little larger, are a good match for group bonsai.

Deep square-shaped containers are suitable for cascade and semi-cascade styles since they emphasize the flexible nature of the plant.

For raft bonsai, long flat containers should be used to give greater energy to the arrangement. Finally, pots for Japanese bonsai are generally supported by fanciful feet that, in addition to raising the pot, make water drainage easier and allow for a certain amount of air circulation.

In the table below we have summarized instructions that you may find useful for properly matching styles to the types of containers available.

SHAPE OF CONTAINER	STYLE FOR WHICH IT IS SUITED
Oval	*Moyogi, hokidachi, ishitsuki, fukinagashi, chokkan, sokan, ikada, yose-ue*
Shallow square shaped	*Moyogi, chokkan, shakan, fukinagashi, hokidachi*
Deep square shaped	*Han-kengai*
Very deep square shaped	*Han-kengai, kengai*
Low, round	*Moyogi, shakan, ishitsuki, bunjingi, fukinagashi, sokan, kabudachi, shankan, hokidachi*
Shallow round	*Moyogi, bunjingi, fukinagashi, shakan, hokidachi*
Very deep round	*Han-kengai, kengai*
Rectangular	*Moyogi, chokkan, hokidachi, ishitsuki, kukinagashi, shakan, yose-ue, kabudachi*
Low in various shapes	*Ikada, yose-ue, hokidachi, netsuranari, kabudachi*

DISEASES AND PESTS

Diseases affecting bonsai are those typical of normal cultivated and wild plants. Compared to the latter, they have fewer natural defenses, but as compensation, the bonsai enthusiast is always watching them closely to quickly take care of the slightest problem.

> *The life of cultivated specimens depends on the ability of the bonsai enthusiast to quickly diagnose a problem and take protective action.*

VIRAL DISEASES

These are undoubtedly among the most dangerous diseases. They are caused by pathogenic viruses whose spread is facilitated by wounds, grazing or insect stings. There are various types of viral diseases, and their danger lies in the difficulty in diagnosing them, and the limited means of treatment available. The most effective weapon we have is **prevention**.

For this reason, we must only deal with trusted nurseries that are able to honestly guarantee the healthy origin of the tiny plant. On our part, we must use clean and disinfected tools for gardening procedures that require the cutting (pruning, trimming, etc.) of plant material in order to avoid the transmission of viral diseases by contact.

The signs of viral diseases include the shortening of internodes on main and minor branches, the tendency of leaves to form clusters, brush-like formations on branches, typical mosaic pigmentation (discolored areas), shriveling and curvature of branch tips.

PESTS

There are many types of pests that attack bonsai. Among the most common are aphids, red and yellow spider mites and scale insects.

▶ Aphids (or green flies) are small insects (approximately 1 mm in size) that live in colonies established primarily on branch tips and leaves where they suck sap and cause branch tips to shrivel and leaf lamina to shorten. In addition, they are able to spread viruses with their sting. They can be removed manually or using chemical pesticides. They can be eliminated biologically using a solution of steeped nettles or dish soap and water.

Aphids are small insects that attack plant shoots and deform them making it easier for viral diseases to spread.

Zelkova nire, approximately 60 years old, trained in the slant style.

The structure shows a good conical form, but the shape of foliage overall requires some correction to fill spaces caused by the lack of small branches.

The size of the lowest branch (the leading branch) must be increased.

of leaves, venation, branches and trunk by sucking their sap. Massive attacks result in serious manifestations of withering that can lead to the plant's death. To combat scale insects, it is advisable to clean plants with small brushes (indeed, scale insects adhere tenaciously to affected areas) together with applications of special-purpose pesticides.

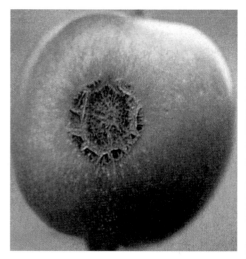

Above: cottony scale insects (the photograph shows a colony that has been enlarged considerably) primarily attack Carmona, Ulmus [elm], Podocarpus, *etc. At right, a small apple affected by scab fungus.*

▶ **Red and yellow spider mites** are miniscule spiders that frequently attack bonsai. They suck the sap from the underside of leaves leaving them speckled.
A massive attack of these pests can result in the complete withering of the plant above ground level, and ultimately death. If there are regular attacks, they can be controlled by using specific acarids that are widely available in specialized stores.

▶ **Scale insects** belong to the homoptera order of insects and are characterized by significant sexual dimorphism; in other words, there are substantial differences between males and females. Females have no wings, almost always have no legs, and show little differentiation between head, thorax and abdomen. By contrast, males usually have wings and legs. The most dangerous scale insects are *diaspis pentagona* and *phillippia oleae*, or the cottony scale insect of the olive tree. These insects form colonies that attack the underside

PLANT-BASED
DISEASES

This type of disease is usually fungal in nature that frequently are in the form of mildew. These diseases are more insidious than pests because of the extremely small size of the infectious agent. As a result, the disease does not manifest itself visually for some time.
There are numerous fungal diseases, but we will limit ourselves to those that most frequently attack bonsai.

▶ Oidium, which is also called powdery mildew, is a fungus with an external mycelium that produces a characteristic white mildew on leaves leading to their weakening and drying.

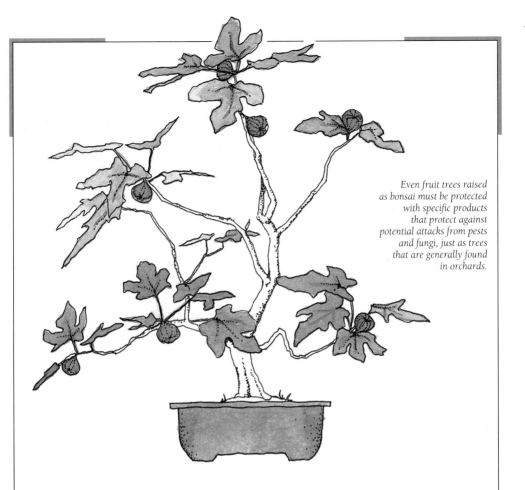

Even fruit trees raised as bonsai must be protected with specific products that protect against potential attacks from pests and fungi, just as trees that are generally found in orchards.

▶ **Scab fungus** or *cladosporiosi*[6] is a fungal disease that takes the form of large patches on the underside of leaves accompanied by gray mildew. The damage caused by scab fungus can be enormous. It can be controlled with copper and calcium oxychloride products.

▶ The **azalea bacteria**, which is a specific fungal agent that attacks, as the name suggests, the azalea plant, attacks flowers and leaves. Initially leaves maintain their natural color, but after a certain period of time, they take on a whitish color that compromises the plant's condition. To treat this disease, all affected areas should be removed immediately.

▶ Finally, ***nectria tumefaciens*** is a fungus that attacks shoots and causes them to die. It can be controlled by pruning all old and diseased branches and promptly removing any areas of infection.

In the tables on the following pages, we have clearly summarized plant care procedures that are necessary for cultivating some of the most widespread species for bonsai.

BONSAI PLANT	PRUNING		WIRE BINDING
	BRANCHES	SHOOTS	
White spruce *Abies alba*	Prune branches before new shoots appear	In the summer when new shoots are about 3 cm long, cut them back to 1 cm.	Year round except during the growth period.
Trident maple *Acer burgeranium*	Slender branches should be pruned before shoots appear, larger ones in the winter.	Trim lateral shoots leaving 2-3 pairs of leaves below. Clip leaves in June	After leaf clipping with plastic-coated wire.
Japanese apricot *Prunus mume*	Prune branches in the spring after flowering.	Trim shoots when fully grown leaving 3-4 buds.	In the summer with plastic-coated wire.
Azalea *Rhododendron lateranium*	Prune young branches leaving 2-3 leaves.	Trim in the summer immediately after flowering. Trim dead leaves in the winter	After flowering with plastic-coated wire.
Birch *Betula nigra*	Prune branches before the appearance of shoots.	Trim new shoots leaving a pair of leaves.	In the summer after trimming.
Cedar of Lebanon *Cedrus libani*	Prune branches before the appearance of shoots.	Trim in the fall leaving two whorls of needles.	Year round.
Quince *Malus baccata*	Prune branches once flowering has ended.	Trim shoots in the spring.	At the end of the summer with plastic-coated wire.
Cotoneaster *Cotoneaster horizontalis*	Prune branches in the spring after flowering.	Trim shoots after flowering.	In the summer with plastic-coated wire.

REPOTTING	WATERING NEEDS	FERTILIZING	OTHER CARE
Every 2 years before shoots appear.	Water regularly; reduce watering when shoots appear.	Once a month from the first sign of buds to October Keep the plant in the shade.	The soil must be slightly acidic.
Every 1-2 years in March before the appearance of shoots.	Regularly with greater frequency in the summer	After buds open, every 20 days until October	Keep in the sun in the spring and fall, and in the shade in summer. Soil must be slightly acidic.
Yearly after flowering.	Water moderately.a	Every 15 days in the spring, and every 20 days in the summer.	Keep the plant in full sun. The soil must be slightly acidic and well drained.
Yearly after flowering.	Water generously while flowering, then maintain moderate moisture.	Fertilize regularly after full flowering until October.	Keep the plant in a bright area in the summer, and near a window in the winter. Soil must be acidic.
Every 2 years, before the appearance of shoots.	Keep soil moist; avoid over watering.	In the summer, once monthly.	Keep the plant in full sun. The soil must be acidic.
Every 2 years before the appearance of shoots	Water regularly.	After the appearance of shoots, once every 3 weeks until October.	Keep the plant in full light. The soil must be acidic.
Yearly before the appearance of shoots.	Water regularly.	Once a week before flowering. Then, every 15 days until October.	Keep the plant in full light. The soil must be somewhat acidic.
Yearly after the appearance of shoots.	Water regularly.	Every 20 days from May to October.	Keep the plant in full sun. The soil must be acidic.

BONSAI PLANT	PRUNING		WIRE BINDING
	BRANCHES	SHOOTS	
Beech *Fagus sylvatica*	*Fagus sylvatica* Prune branches in the spring before new shoots appear, or in October.	Trim shoots in June and July leaving a couple of leaves.	After trimming.
Gardenia *Gardenia jasminoides*	Prune branches before the appearance of shoots.	Trim flowers leaving 2-3 pairs of leaves. Repeat in summer leaving 2-3 leaves.	In the middle of summer.
Juniper *Juniperus communis*	Prune branches in the spring or fall.	As needed, trim back two thirds of shoots until the fall.	In March or October.
Ginkgo *Ginkgo biloba*	Prune branches in the spring before the appearance of buds.	Trim shoots leaving 3-4 leaves.	After trimming leaves, with plastic-coated wire.
Magnolia *Magnolia stellata*	Prune branches in the spring before the appearance of shoots.	Trim after flowering and leave a pair of leaves.	In the summer after trimming.
Pomegranate *Punica granatum*	Prune larger branches in the summer.	Trim from April to June.	In the summer, with plastic-coated wire
Pine *Pinus sylvestris*	Prune branches in the spring or fall.	Trim in the summer removing shoots with fingertips.	In the fall or winter.
Zelkova *Zelkova serrata*	Prune branches in the spring after flowering.	Continually trim shoots until July.	In the summer, with plastic-coated wire.

REPOTTING	WATERING NEEDS	FERTILIZING	OTHER CARE
Every 2-3 years before shoots appear	Water regularly.	Once a month from the first sign of shoots to October	Keep the plant in full sun. The soil must be slightly acidic.
Every 2 years before the appearance of shoots.	Water generously during flowering; then maintain a constant level of moisture.	Once a month all summer and the beginning of the fall.	Keep the plant in the shade. The soil must be slightly acidic.
Every 2 years in March-April before the appearance of shoots.	Water when the soil is dry.	Once a month from March to May and from July to September.	Keep the plant in full sun to obtain small needles. The soil must be slightly acidic.
Every 3-4 years in the spring before the appearance of shoots.	Water regularly.	Once a month from March to the end of June.	Keep the plant in full sun. The soil must be slightly acidic and well drained.
Every year, before the appearance of shoots.	Water moderately with greater regularity in the summer.	Once a month after flowering until October.	Keep the plant in full sun. The soil must be acidic.
Every 2 years before the appearance of shoots	Water regularly.	Once a week until flowering.	Keep the plant in full sun. The soil must be slightly acidic.
Every 2 years before the appearance of shoots, or in the fall.	Water regularly.	Once a month from February to October.	Keep the plant in full sun to obtain small needles. The soil must be somewhat acidic.
Every 2 years after the appearance of shoots.	Water regularly.	Once a month from March to October.	Keep the plant in full sun. The soil must be slightly acidic.

To correct excessively straight bifurcation of the trunk, pruning will be needed to decrease vegetation.

A good specimen of Quercus ilex [holly oak], a resistant and robust species that was found in nature. Using this basic structure the plant can be trained in the upside-down broom or formal upright style.

Base of trunk – The realistic effect of the base of the trunk makes the bonsai particularly agreeable.

Leaves – The minute size of leaves of this variety makes it particularly suitable for bonsai treatment.

Printing completed in May 2002